✔ KU-193-848

You're so Smart, Snoopy

Charles M. Schulz

Selected cartoons from
You're out of sight, Charlie Brown, Vol 1

CORONET BOOKS
Hodder Fawcett, London

Copyright © 1970 by United Feature Syndicate Inc.

Peanuts comic strips copyright © 1969, 1970
by United Feature Syndicate Inc.

This book, prepared especially for Fawcett Publications,
Inc., comprises the first half of YOU'RE OUT OF SIGHT
CHARLIE BROWN, and is reprinted by arrangement
with Holt, Rinehart & Winston, Inc.

First published in 1974 by Fawcett Publications Inc.

Coronet edition 1976
Seventh impression 1980

Printed in Great Britain for Hodder
Fawcett Ltd., Mill Road, Dunton Green,
Sevenoaks, Kent. (Editorial Office:
47 Bedford Square, London, WC1 3DP) by
C. Nicholls & Company Ltd.
The Philips Park Press, Manchester

ISBN 0 340 19927 X

I WANT TO MAKE MY OWN VALENTINES THIS YEAR, BUT I CAN'T DRAW A GOOD HEART

TRY DRAWING JUST ONE SIDE, AND THEN FOLD IT OVER AND TRACE THE OTHER SIDE

FOLD IT OVER?! I HATE FOLDING THINGS OVER! WHY DOES IT HAVE TO BE SO COMPLICATED?

FOLD! CUT! CREASE! TEAR! MEASURE! TRACE! DRAW! FORGET IT! FORGET IT, I SAY! FORGET IT!!!

I WONDER WHAT IT WOULD BE LIKE TO GET A VALENTINE FROM SOMEONE YOU LIKED AND WHO REALLY LIKED YOU...

I WONDER WHAT IT WOULD BE LIKE TO NEVER FIND OUT..

THE PRINCIPAL'S OFFICE? YES, MA'AM..

NOW, WHAT IN THE WORLD DOES THE PRINCIPAL WANT TO SEE **ME** ABOUT? MAYBE HE WANTS ME TO MANAGE THE SCHOOL BALL TEAM THIS NEXT SEASON...I DOUBT IT..

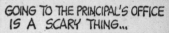

GOING TO THE PRINCIPAL'S OFFICE IS A SCARY THING...

I THINK THEY PURPOSELY PUT THE DOOR KNOB UP HIGH TO MAKE YOU FEEL INFERIOR!

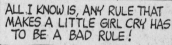

THE WHOLE
THING WAS
KIND OF
WEIRD..

THIS CAT WAS ABOUT
THREE FEET TALL, SEE,
AND HE..

I REALLY SHOULD HAVE SOME PHOTOGRAPHS IN MY FAN MAGAZINE TO GIVE IT SOME CLASS, BUT I DON'T KNOW HOW TO PRINT THEM...

LAST YEAR JOE BATTED .143 AND MADE SOME SPECTACULAR CATCHES OF ROUTINE FLY BALLS. HE ALSO THREW OUT A RUNNER WHO HAD FALLEN DOWN BETWEEN FIRST AND SECOND.

WELL, FANS, THERE IT IS. REMEMBER, THIS LITTLE OL' FAN MAGAZINE IS YOURS. WE WELCOME YOUR COMMENTS.

WHO NEEDS IT?

I SHOULDN'T HAVE WELCOMED HER COMMENTS...

SCHULZ

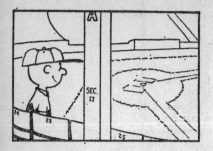

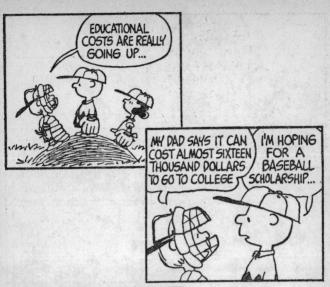

POW!

THAT'S THE LONGEST HOME RUN EVER HIT IN THIS PARK, CHARLIE BROWN, AND YOU WERE THE PITCHER..

THAT MEANS YOUR NAME WILL GO DOWN IN THE RECORD BOOKS

LOOK UNDER "GOAT"

YOU DID IT!! YOU REPORTED SNOOPY TO THE HEAD BEAGLE!

IT WAS HIS OWN FAULT! HE NEVER WANTED TO GO RABBIT CHASING WITH ME!

SHE REPORTED ME, AND NOW I HAVE TO APPEAR BEFORE THE HEAD BEAGLE..THIS WILL BRING DISGRACE UPON THE DAISY HILL PUPPY FARM...

IN ALL THE HISTORY OF THE DAISY HILL PUPPY FARM, NO ONE HAS EVER BEEN ORDERED TO APPEAR BEFORE THE HEAD BEAGLE!!

EVERYONE IS MAD AT ME..NO ONE WILL SPEAK TO ME...

OF COURSE, THEY WON'T! ANYONE WHO WOULD TURN SOMEONE IN TO THE HEAD BEAGLE DOESN'T DESERVE TO BE SPOKEN TO!

I DIDN'T KNOW WHAT I WAS DOING! I WAS UPSET!

DON'T TALK TO ME..IT'S TOO LATE NOW!

HERE'S THE DOOMED DEFENDANT DRESSED IN BLACK ON HIS WAY TO APPEAR BEFORE THE HEAD BEAGLE...

HE'S BACK! SNOOPY'S BACK!

HE LOOKS KIND OF DAZED, CHARLIE BROWN...

THIS IS THE WAY YOU ALWAYS LOOK WHEN YOU RETURN FROM HAVING APPEARED BEFORE THE HEAD BEAGLE!

It was a dark and stormy night.

Suddenly, a shot rang out. A door slammed. The maid screamed.

Suddenly, a pirate ship appeared on the horizon!

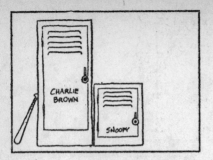

GOOD GRIEF, IT'S ALMOST NOON!

WE HAVE TO SUIT-UP FOR THE BALL GAME, SNOOPY..

OKAY, LET'S SHOW A LITTLE LIFE OUT THERE!

?

HEY, MANAGER...SOME KID MUST HAVE LEFT HIS GLOVE HERE... IT HAS HIS NAME ON IT..

TWO HUNDRED TO NOTHING!! GOOD GRIEF!

HOW CAN WE LOSE TWO HUNDRED TO NOTHING? WHAT HAPPENED?

I THOUGHT IF WE ALL DRANK THAT BALANCED ELECTROLYTE SOLUTION, WE'D WIN.... WHAT HAPPENED?!

MAYBE WE DRANK TOO MUCH THE FIRST INNING...

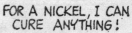

Part II
A light snow was falling, and the little girl with the tattered shawl had not sold a violet all day.

At that very moment, a young intern at City Hospital was making an important discovery.

I MAY HAVE WRITTEN MYSELF INTO A CORNER...

It was a dark and stormy night. Suddenly a shot rang out. A door slammed. The maid screamed.

Suddenly a pirate ship appeared on the horizon. While millions of people were starving, the king lived in luxury. Meanwhile, on a small farm in Kansas, a boy was growing up.
End of Part I

Part II.... A light snow was falling, and the little girl with the tattered shawl had not sold a violet all day.

At that very moment, a young intern at City Hospital was making an important discovery. The mysterious patient in Room 213 had finally awakened. She moaned softly.

Could it be that she was the sister of the boy in Kansas who loved the girl with the tattered shawl who was the daughter of the maid who had escaped from the pirates? The intern frowned.

SEE HOW NEATLY ALL OF THIS FITS TOGETHER?

BUT WHAT ABOUT THE KING?

BONK!

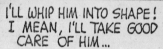

WELL, HOW WAS YOUR VACATION, CHARLIE BROWN?

VACATIONS ARE DREADED, SUFFERED, ENDURED, TOLERATED, SPOILED, RUINED AND WASTED...

VACATIONS CAN BE GREAT, TERRIBLE, WONDERFUL, AWFUL, DELIGHTFUL AND STUPID

I SPENT MY WHOLE VACATION WORRYING ABOUT MY DOG..

YOU NEED A VACATION, CHARLIE BROWN!

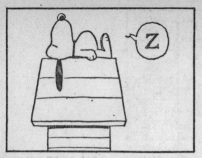

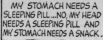

It was a dark and stormy night. Suddenly, a shot rang out!

The maid screamed. A door slammed.

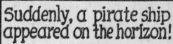

Suddenly, a pirate ship appeared on the horizon!

THIS TWIST IN THE PLOT WILL BAFFLE MY READERS...